The Gaze of Love

SISTER WENDY BECKETT

The Gaze of Love

MEDITATIONS ON ART

Marshall Pickering
An Imprint of HarperCollins*Publishers*

Marshall Pickering is an Imprint of
HarperCollins*Religious*
Part of HarperCollins*Publishers*
77–85 Fulham Palace Road, London W6 8JB

First published in Great Britain
in 1993 by Marshall Pickering

1 3 5 7 9 10 8 6 4 2

A catalogue record for this book is
available from the British Library

ISBN 0 551 02810-6

Photoset in Linotron Bembo by
Rowland Phototypesetting Limited, Bury St Edmunds, Suffolk

Printed and bound in Great Britain by
Butler & Tanner Limited, Frome, Somerset

The publishers would like to thank
SISTER MARGARET SHERIDAN S. N. D.
for her invaluable help and generosity.

CONTENTS

Introduction

Acknowledgements

INTRODUCTION

BOOKS ON PRAYER ARE DANGEROUS. They take time to read and they demand attention. This is proof, is it not (says our subconscious), that we are serious, spiritual people? Does not our very choice of reading matter, the interest we take in prayer, differentiate us from the careless, the frivolous, the less committed? The answer is no. At some level that we do not recognize, we may well be reading books on prayer as a way to allay our guilt about not actually praying. The overweight, it is said, are devoted readers of diet books, the sedentary devour travel books. Reading about prayer, talking about prayer, even writing about prayer: these are not useless activities but they are dangerous.

The real difficulty about prayer is that it has no difficulty. Prayer is God's taking possession of us. We expose to Him what we are, and He gazes on us with the creative eye of Holy Love. His gaze is transforming: He does not leave us in our poverty but draws into being all we are meant to become. What that is we can never know. Total Love sees us in total truth because it is only He who sees us totally. Nobody else can ever know us through and through, know why we are what we are, what inherited weaknesses and strengths we have, or what wounds or insights have come to us from our upbringing. We may think we know many of these, but we are often mistaken. We must all have had the embarrassing experience of listening to friends detail their own characteristics, and known that their verdict is not objectively true. We see one another's unconscious self-deceptions, but we may not be as aware of our own. It is not only our faults we may overlook, but – perhaps even more – our virtues. There is a certain satisfaction in thinking ill of ourselves, both in that it confirms us in a hope of our lack of conceit, and in that it flatters our laziness. A gift always means we have to work with it, and so we may prefer not to be overtly aware of our own potential. But none of these escapes are possible if we pray. God sees us in our absolute truth, and seeing us, He loves us and brings us to blissful fulfilment.

How God gazes at us is not our business. We are only asked to allow Him to take possession. We cannot hasten or control this state. Certainly a response is called for, but what that is to be is something that only the individual at prayer can know. There are no norms, no rules, no prohibitions, or at least, none as such. What "rules" there are arise spontaneously in the act of prayer. All prayer demands that we look at God, (which usually means that we look into "nothingness", God being pure Spirit and unconfinable in any image), and do what seems to work. Whether our response is working or not – whether it is a way into love or an escape into self – only we can know. If it seems right, it will be right, God being bound by His own honour to make it clear to us if we are mistaken. We can see that prayer is based wholly on being truthful. If we want God to be our all, then we shall want to do whatever pleases Him. Prayer is the only human action or state where cheating is impossible. As soon as pretence sets in, prayer stops. It never wholly stops since God never ceases looking at us with love, but He needs our consent if His love is not to be powerless. It is precisely this total freedom in prayer that we find so appalling. We long to be safe behind a barricade of methods, all protecting us from our own weakness, but in this very protection, shutting us off from God. It is the real self with all its weakness that He desires. He cannot transform us if we insist on only offering to Him our goodness, our successes, our strengths. Controlled prayer is only partial prayer: it is the giving up the control to God that makes prayer true.

If we give up control and abandon methods, what do we actually do at prayer? This question is rather like asking what husbands and wives say to each other. There is no one answer, since each couple is different and they live together through different stages of their marriage. The only certainty is that a good marriage depends upon one real person responding to another. God is supremely real: the problem is our own unreality. How do we overcome it? If willing were enough, we could spring free with a single bound, but we do not even understand the depth of our interior falsehood, let alone its areas or how to eradicate them. But God does: making us real is the effect of prayer, just as it is its accompaniment. We seek to be true when we pray, to do whatever we feel will most yield us up to God. What that may be will differ for each. One person may find it sets her free if she sings, another if he slowly reads a line of scripture. One may want to say the name of Jesus, breathing gently in and out, another may find it helps to have an imaginary scene of the gospels in mind. Some may want nothing, just to reach up to that cloud of unknowing in which and through which we come to the Mystery of God. There are obviously things we can and should do before we pray, such as enter into silence for short periods during the day, just resting on God, as it were. It helps to read theology that makes practical sense (which is not true of all theological books); we need to read and reread the Scriptures; we are madly foolish if we have access to the sacraments and do not use them. But this is remote preparation; our concern here and now is the actual time we set aside to grow in truth, to receive love, in other words, to pray.

For some people, a help towards this is to make use of art. It can anchor the mind and serve as a jumping-off place, too, to mix metaphors. The idea would be to look at the picture and read the commentary before the

ALBERT HERBERT *Moses on the Mountain of God*, 1991
Oil on canvas, 51 x 61 cm

actual time of prayer, and then keep the book open, so that every time one looks again at the image, desire springs up afresh and we are centred. But if there are no "rules" except those that are functional, then there is no reason why the pictures and commentaries should not be used as prayer itself. This could be an escape from the solitariness of prayer, the unsupported confrontation with Holiness. But it could be a means to this confrontation: only the individual can tell.

Very few of the pictures in this book are religious or uncontemporary. The omissions are deliberate. When we look at a religious picture we all too easily take refuge in its theology, imposing patterns that are comforting but perhaps lead us nowhere. There are very few contemporary artists who use religious imagery. This is not a matter of what the artists want to do but what they are able to do. True art comes from so deep in the psyche that it almost forces itself out. The images come, not from the artists, but through them, so to speak. So it is not a question of faith or desire which many contemporaries have, but one of necessity. Albert Herbert, probably the greatest of contemporary religious artists, fought for years against his longing to paint biblical themes, until he came to realize that this, for him, was fulfilment. It is not the subject itself that makes his work so powerful, because many lesser artists have taken the same subject and given us more or less skilful illustrations of it. Religious art does not "illustrate", or not primarily. What it does is to carry us away from the limitations of what we already know and believe and set us free in the infinities of a deeper vision. When Herbert paints *Moses on the Mountain of God* he involves us in the experience of setting out, frail and lonely, upon the painful and arduous business of a step by weary step ascent towards an unseen God. Moses is stripped, intent upon his end. St John of the Cross, talking about the mystical mountain, wrote that

RAPHAEL (1483–1520) *Altarpiece: The Madonna and Child with
Saint John the Baptist and Saint Nicholas of Bari (The Ansidei Madonna)*
Wood, arched top, painted area 209.5 x 148.5 cm

GUERCINO (1591–1666) *The Woman taken in Adultery*
Oil on canvas, 98.2 x 122.7 cm

there is nothing, nothing, nothing on the way, and on the mountain – nothing. Moses perseveres because he believes, because God matters immensely to him and he needs no proof of God's goodness. He goes on behalf of all the big-egoed people who stand at the bottom and watch from afar. He ascends for everyone, and his lonely cloudy encounter will be for us all. Herbert conveys the whole dramaless drama of the spiritual ascent in his small and exquisite painting, and its very originality and personal intensity make it easier for us to see what it expresses. Herbert slips past our preconceptions in the way that a more traditional painter may be unable to do. The Old Masters come burdened with their fame and familiarity. Before we even start to respond spiritually to a great Raphael we have to contend with our knowledge that we are looking at a masterpiece. It is almost impossible to see with an innocent eye a paint-ing like the *Ansidei Madonna*, one of the great Raphaels in the National Gallery. It shows the Virgin and Child with two saints, St John the Baptist, looking yearningly upwards, and St Nicholas of Bari, a quiet scholarly bishop, lost in his reading. The sheer majesty of the painting is almost daunting: this is "great art". We need to work out the significance of the attendant saints and break through the barriers of respect before we are able really to enjoy the tender sweetness of the young Mary with her rosebud mouth and roseleaf complexion, holding with such happy confidence the curled figure of her drowsy Son. It is a wonderful painting, very apt for prolonged prayerful gazing, but both fame and time set it at a little distance. Our Lady may seem too remote to be immediately access-ible, and the sheer beauty of both saints, perfect in their every aspect as seemed only appropriate to Raphael, may distance them from the very unperfect viewer. This is not at all to suggest that we cannot use the Old Masters for our prayer – far from it. But it may be easier to start on art

REMBRANDT (1606–1669) *The Woman taken in Adultery*, 1644
Oil on wood (oak) top corners rounded, 83.8 x 65.4 cm

that comes across to us with what Robert Hughes has called "the shock of the new".

The centre of our religion is Jesus. He is the only man who has looked into the cloud, seen with His own eyes the Face of the holy mystery, and turned round to assure us that the name of God is "Father". Jesus had a real material face and artists throughout the ages have sought to portray it. The Old Masters bring to this portrayal all their genius, and we have as yet no modern painter who we can acclaim with certainty as their equal. Yet even here, the contemporary artist has what we could call a functional advantage. The Dulwich Art Gallery has one of the most beautiful depictions of Christ ever painted: Guercino's *The Woman taken in Adultery*. Jesus regards the sinner with a grave compassion, and the tension, the meeting together of hopes and fears, are mostly conveyed by hands. The woman's hands are folded in despairing resignation: she is locking herself into herself, away from the agonies of her situation. One accuser holds her with white-knuckled force, condemning her in his justification for his own failings. The venerable chief accuser stretches out one elegant long-fingered hand in contempt. He is using the woman as an object, a "thing" on which to hang his theology. The other hand is that of the preacher or teacher, counting off on his fingers the points against his victim. These two hands are central; this is where the human passion is. Jesus looks deep into the eyes of his impressive opponent. He makes one small gesture, also pointing towards the woman, but with infinite understanding. We remember how the story ends, with Jesus challenging anyone who is without sin, to throw the "first stone" at their fellow sinner. When the woman, braced for her death by stoning, looks up, she will find herself alone with Jesus and be gently told to go in peace and sin no more. Even Rembrandt, with his marvellous picture in the

National Gallery, with the actors in the drama spotlit amidst the immense darkness of the temple, does not convey the wonder of divine forgiveness as does Guercino. Yet, despite all this, even such a work may present a difficulty. Just as the Catholic use of Latin in the Mass could suggest, subliminally, that we need a special language with which to talk to God, so might even a painting as tender as this suggest that Jesus lived in what I can only call "fancy-dress times". Ludicrous though it sounds, neither the clothes nor, still more, the faces of Guercino's seventeenth-century Bologna are wholly assimilable to twentieth-century Europe or America. This is not our world. We can most definitely enter into Guercino's world and find God in it, but for some people this is an added burden. For sheer practicality, therefore, most of the paintings in this book are contemporary. Since contemporary art is for the most part secular, the images are in consequence mostly non-religious too.

Paradoxically, this has an inbuilt advantage. With a religious image we feel we know in advance how to react. The artist may be able to circumvent our expectations by the sheer passion of his vision. Michael Finn's *Crucifix* (which he made for his son's ordination as a priest) has a raw emotion that affects us even before we have our reverence ready. His Christ is such a pitiful figure, so disintegrated, so dehumanized by pain, "A worm and no man". Finn's Redeemer is as disjointed and lifeless as any poor dead human being can be, and he jolts us by the ordinariness and underemphasis of his image into a new awareness of what Jesus is and what his death means to us. These jolts, wrecking our complacencies and wrenching us into fresh insights, are always at hand in the great non-religious images of major artists. A painting like Anne Grebby's *Ashes* will not let us pigeonhole it away from our consciousness. We are forced by its strangeness to come to some sort of terms, to try to let it

MICHAEL FINN *Crucifix*, 1985/6
Painted gesso on wood, 147 x 99 cm

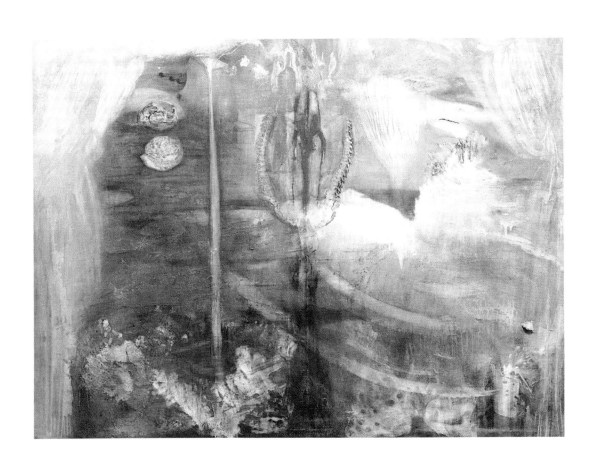

ANNE GREBBY *Ashes*, 1992
Oil on canvas, 152 x 203 cm

open up within us and "communicate". Its passionate beauty, with that richly coloured central shape pulsing with blood red significance, makes us want to "understand", yet the answers are clearly not verbal. Grebby says that she is "trying to reveal living connections . . . without so much of my own intervention . . . no juxtapositions, ambiguities, no clues . . . just things". She adds: "flow and flux . . . and some gaps in between", and she quotes William Blake's famous lines about "the doors of perception". If they "were cleansed, everything would appear to man as it is – infinite". Blake believed that we have shut ourselves up, so that we can only see "all things through narrow chinks" in our imprisoning "cavern". This cleansing of the doors of perception requires great vigilance – we must wholeheartedly desire it, and Grebby speaks of not "making do with any of our conditionings, which succeed in limiting us daily to the containment of the world". *Ashes* is an artist's attempt to escape that "containment", to clear the debris from the eyes of the spirit, (the "doors of perception"), so that we may see the infinite in the ordinary. Infinity cannot be circumscribed by word or image, but it can be experienced in the mystery of an artist's painting. With nothing to cling onto in such a painting, we may be set free into the freedom of the children of God.

When Lino Mannocci paints the Annunciation, that sacred moment that changed the course of human history, that spelt out for us our sacred destiny, he does not use the traditional imagery. He paints *Isle of the Annunciation*, and we are faced with a great blue sea, white-flecked and heaving, on which floats an "isle" – a small rectangular raft. We can see the angel, but where is the Virgin? He speaks from the cloud, never touching our sea-bound earth, and he addresses his Ave to a flower, bending low in awe, while the heavens coalesce into a white radiance that will soon "overshadow" her. The unconventionality of Mannocci's vision

LINO MANNOCCI *Isle of the Annunciation*, 1991
Oil on canvas, 35 × 50 cm

forces us into a new understanding of what is happening, and the loveliness of his colour keeps us silent within the radiance that he calls into being. Even when there is no abstraction (as in Anne Grebby's *Ashes*), or surrealist originality (as in Lino Mannocci's *Isle of the Annunciation*), but only what seems straightforward landscape, a great contemporary artist can speak to us of the Spirit and deepen our capacity for prayer. When Peter Prendergast paints *Dinefwr: Spring*, the leaping, rushing brightness of his painting gives us so profound a sense of what spring is, that we go through the material image into that springtime of the heart that Jesus envisages when he wishes us "life, life to the full". The interior vitality that is the effect of divine closeness is not the subject of Prendergast's picture, but that free, sweet exuberance is an earthly counterpart of spiritual exultation, and the one mirrors the other. Prayer is never meant to be confined to a "time of prayer". We need these times, when we set all aside and surrender to God's presence, but at all times we are called to be with Him. Work and daily concerns make that awareness something at the back of our minds, but without that continual secret presence, we are diminished. Prayer is like an underground stream that flows to the surface at the times when we can give it undiverted space. Art that is not specifically religious expresses this truth: if we do not see the Lord everywhere, however unconsciously, we shall find it hard to recognize Him when we look into His face at prayer time.

In a sense, art is deeply compatible with the Incarnation. "No one has ever seen God", who is essentially unseeable. But we do see Him in Jesus. Jesus is the humble human image of the Invisible Holy One. He is God in human terms, and the longer and more intently we contemplate His life, the more we shall come to "know the Father". (Even an impenetrable mystery, like the power in our lives of evil, is answered by the life of

PETER PRENDERGAST *Dinefwr: Spring*, 1991
Oil on canvas, 62.5 x 92 cm

Jesus. "Why does God allow it?", we cry. Looking at the crucified Christ, we can see that, whatever the "reason", God is not indifferent to our agonies. When He became man, He shared them and He made them redemptive. We do not have a God "out there", but one intimately close, flesh of our flesh, and the very materiality of art can make that evident.)

The contents of this book are not meant to be read at a sitting. The intention is that only one be read at a time, ideally, each of the forty days of Lent, and the painting savoured, dwelt upon, used. The actual reflections opposite each are really only to keep one within the presence of the art. Every reader will have his or her own commentaries, far more apposite to their personal state than mine. There may be no need of any words: the art may work its effect in silence. Abstract art in particular often seems to be vulgarized by verbalizing. But the pictures will only work to the extent that we wish them to work. If we fear the truth, if we are essentially reluctant to see what we have innocently hidden from ourselves, then nothing can open our eyes. We are all blind to some degree (and none more than I myself!). But if we want to pray, then we shall pray. There is nothing whatever that can hold us back. Naked desire meets naked God, and nobody on earth can intervene with suggestions or advice. Pictures may not work for you: then enjoy them for the art, out of prayer-time. At some level, if there is enjoyment, they are, in fact, working. We have a thrifty God who lets nothing that is good within us ever go to waste.

The Gaze of Love

Odilon Redon

"We enter God's energy when we pray."

At first we hardly see the sailor, still less that she has a companion. Both are lost, hidden, secret within the boat's blueness, the colour of heaven. The two – because the mystic heart is never alone, an angelic Presence, the hidden God, is always with her – do not steer the boat, do not even try to direct it. They sit surrendered, allowing the Spirit to take them where He chooses. The sea is not still for the one who prays, it heaves and is turbulent, but the tossing of the boat is part of the mystic journey. It is the outward stress that makes the surrender of trust vital. The sail alone catches the full brightness of God, and it is that brightness, overhead, not tangible, that dominates the picture. But the brightness blinds the sailor, she cannot see where the Spirit is taking her, and she leans back, at rest, content in His spiritual choice. It is not in the minutiae of daily living that she abandons choice, but in her prayer. The daily living is the choppy sea, but her prayer is the deep faithful blue of the boat, the bright loving gold of its sail, all that bears her forward in a power not her own.

Pastel and black chalk on buff-coloured wove paper, 54.4 × 67.5 cm

Margaret Neve

ANGEL IN THE SKY, 1987

"Our function is to contain the radiance of Light."

Using tiny specks of pure colour, Margaret Neve builds up scenes that have a sort of subliminal luminosity. The light is so subtle that it can appear almost drab at first sight. Here an angel flies through an evening sky. (Evening rather than morning because the shepherd is leading home his flock.) Heaven is all subdued pinks and blues, earth – and here we pause – and look again. Earth is the same pink and blue, but in different proportions. Those rounding fields, dotted with more and more incident the more we look, those trees and bushes and houses and sheds, those rivers and haystacks and sheep with their shepherd – all are an inwardly glowing pink-blue. The angel in the sky expresses these colours fully, we could say more absolutely, but heaven and earth are profoundly alike.

Do we allow our own personal earth to be heaven? Do we see, in faith, that God in His beauty is as intimately our own as we choose Him to be? How freely do we let soak deep into our being His radiance? And seek it within, where it truly is?

The angel is no glamorous figure. He is a stocky stony angel, but his great virtue is that he is wholly intent. Every angelic sinew, every feather in his great pinions, is soberly concentrated on his task. We are not told here what that task may be. The position of his hands suggests an annunciation, but the angel looks neither to right nor left, neither down nor up. He moves steadily towards his God-given mission. The angel knows where he is going, and whomever he visits will receive the divine message without having to search for the messenger. There is a sense in which the angel is always coming, motionless overhead. At God's time he will speak God's word. Our part is to live in the heaven of God's invisible Presence so that we can hear and see when our sacred summons arrives. And we can also say that it has arrived, is arriving, will arrive. The angel is permanent in our sky if we live in the truth of Jesus.

Oil on wood panel, 48 × 51 cm

Maria Chevska

LIVING MEMORY (DIPTYCH), 1988

"With God we never initiate, only respond."

If we know Maria Chevska's previous work, which is essentially figurative, *Living Memory* can come as a disconcerting new approach. We seem to be faced with a canvas in two parts, both equally baffling. Yet this is clearly not abstract art in the usual sense. We may not find a "meaning", a "reading", yet one tugs at our memory, pushes up against our consciousness, proclaims some secret importance. On the left we see – what? A delicate cloth hanging from a branch or a bare back? A tent, half-fallen? A rag and a bone? These strange faint shapes come from an ancestral memory so deep that we cannot pull it into the light of the labelling intellect. And beside, on the right, we see at first a tender medley of colour and shape which only gradually takes on the memory of a cave wall, a Lascaux cave with its active and vital animal shapes appearing and disappearing into its recesses. Both panels suggest age, concealments, protections, that secret world within to which we do not have free access.

But God has access. All our mysteries not only lie open to Him but only find their meaning and their beauty in Him. By her reverent attention to memory that is alive and life that is remembered, Chevska acts out for us, draws from herself and from the silent viewer, the state of prayer. She exposes, not what she knows she is, but what she does not know but can merely, vaguely, secretly, intuit, and she exposes this to God. His silent Presence validates the viewer's (and the artist's) silence: we are swept beyond our narrow certainties into the freedom of infinite truth. And yet to verbalize all this is at once to diminish its power. If we are to live in God and be remembered in Him, we have to sacrifice the self-importance of control and explicit explanations. All we need to do here is to contemplate.

This need to keep silence is significant. Both sides of the diptych, one so pale and fragile, one so many-hued and enduring, unite into a single whole. If these diverse elements of the one interior reality are to become significant for us, drawing us into their wholeness, it entails allowing all of our being, all its potential and actuality, good or bad, clear or unknown, chosen or involuntary, to be seen by God and made whole. Our past (memory) and our present (living) lie open in prayer before Him.

Wax and oil on canvas, 91.5 × 183 cm

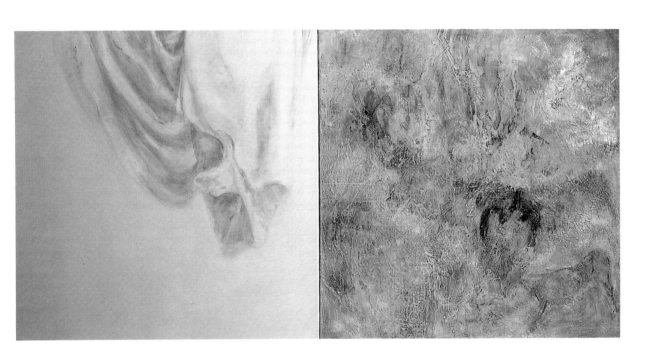

Maxwell Doig

WELDING MASK BEHIND METAL
PLATE I AND II, 1991

"Surrender the proof – this is faith."

Maxwell Doig's two "welding masks" stare grimly out at us. They are "metal plates", masks not to conceal but to protect, masks that enable a task to be achieved, and in this context, it would seem implied that it is a creative task. The welding masks are used in their own making.

They make a contrasting pair. *Mask I* is metal colour still, the red–hot fire just beginning to flush its stiffness. The centre is an opaque rectangle. But *Mask II* is a blazing crimson; even the visor of the centre has melted into another shape.

The masks are the same, yet different, not quite before and after – more like two variations of the theme of mask and function. Doig makes us ponder the meaning of a mask, and the risks of a welder.

If we wear masks as we go about our daily business, is it for some serious and worthy purpose, like the welder, or are we escaping from some weakness? Are we afraid to show our true face? What does love ask of us? *Mask I* is grim, intent, tense. It is worn only so that the welding may take place, and the object to be welded is one that matters. To join together in a welded form is a solemn obligation. In one way or another, all human creatures must weld and be welded: we are never meant to live without love relationship.

But we see from Doig's *Metal Plate* that this welding is costly. We cannot do it without labour, without prayer, without the urge of strong desire. *Mask II* tells us that the welding is also an affair of passion. Desire must engross us, we must intensely choose. The two go together, the intent choice, the passion, and the action chosen, the deed.

We will only have the energy and commitment for the work if we think out our motivations and go steadfastly ahead. Doig plays with the lovely geometry of his forms: the rectangle and the oval superimposed on each other and slipping in and out of focus. The seriousness is a matter of celebration as well as of labour. The two images sing, they bear the weight of their meaning with gentle authority. At the one margin, each is abruptly curtailed, as though continuing out into infinity, while at the other margin, they neighbour each other and eternity: Doig refers us to and draws us to contemplating interaction.

Mixed media, 50 × 63 cm

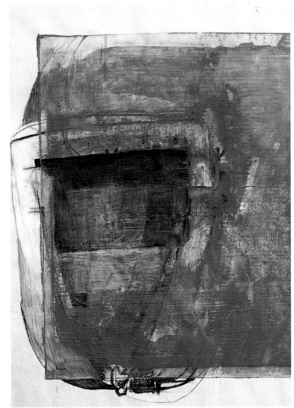

Albert Marquet

SAILING BOATS AT LA ROCHELLE, 1920

"Eternity is only found in the NOW."

Marquet was a lifelong friend of Matisse and an early Fauve, both factors that contributed to his complete and contented awareness of being only minor in comparison. He often painted the same scenes as Matisse, and the absence of the power of great genius is very marked. Yet, being minor is also a vocation! Marquet consistently gives pleasure, his work is so charming, so truthful, so pure even, in its humble sweetness. I find these little boats on their calm water a moving picture. It makes no demands, as all the great ones do, it simply rejoices and shares. Passion is a precious gift, and so too is acceptance of limitation, its necessary counterfoil. Small boats on a small bay, dun skies, muted water: the freedom of the humble soul that is content to be as He chooses.

Oil on canvas, 45 × 45 cm

Robert Natkin

HITCHCOCK SERIES – EGYPT, 1988

"The Egypt heart is not synonymous with the ego-cock;
it is the creative, potential side of us."

Robert Natkin's Hitchcock Series takes its rise from his great admiration for this film maker who takes the seemingly superficial, the stuff of the thriller and cheap magazine, and shows it to be electric with significance. Hitchcock keeps the familiar form but he explodes it into beauty, terror and the symbolic longings most deeply rooted in the human heart. Something of this same intention irradiates Natkin's own work. He shows us nothing strange, nothing that looks difficult. *Egypt* offers us a softly glowing network of pinks, greens, yellows, blues melting into one another, too inwardly luminous to be rightly described by the bareness of nouns, a sort of heavenly mesh that holds light before us, weighted down at the edges by solid chunks of colour, held in a rich variable frame, somehow present and yet quivering on the verge of dissolving in the hidden light from within.

Like a Hitchcock story, this seems on one level a simple picture – Natkin can appear too beautiful to be "demanding". But, like Hitchcock, this is deceptive. The simple beauty has layers upon layers of secret significance. What exactly that significance is, is something too deep to be expressed in the boxes of speech. *Egypt* is a gateway, not to Egypt the country, but to the Egypt of the heart. We recall its mysteriously majestic art, its aura of exotic secrecy, pyramids, tombs, the Nile and its gods. We recall the Jewish captivity there, Moses and the parting of the Red Sea, the Flight there of the Holy Family, its use in later writings as a symbol of human luxury – the fleshpots of Egypt. It is the non-puritan country, one where man is never in control but is also mysteriously fulfilled. It is a symbol of all within us that we fear or feel ashamed of: the loneliness of the desert, the cruelty of the slave-owner, the dependence on the Nile, the secrets hidden in the sand of the subconscious, strange gods and strange visions. We both fear our Egypt selves and seek to repress them. Yet God cannot make us holy unless we are present to Him in our whole truth. Egypt is part of our global reality. Pretending it is not there simply cuts it off from God's transforming love. Like this supremely beautiful Natkin, we cannot fathom the "meaning", but we intuit its mystical presence. We enter more and more deeply into the sheer "thereness" of the painting. So do we enter, with grace, into the sheer truth of our being: we expose it *all* to God, and He will make our Egypt His Land.

Acrylic on canvas, 122 × 183 cm

Ken Kiff

FLOWER AND BLACK SKY, 1987–88

*"One meaning of life is for us to orchestrate creation
to His praise."*

Here, if ever, is a picture to be contemplated rather than discussed. It scarcely seems to have made it into material existence. One side of the paper is ragged and torn, and the edges wobble as if under the pressure of Ken Kiff's emotion. The flower stands alone in a lifeless landscape. To the left is a skeletal tree, pale green like an enlarged branch of seaweed, waving its dead branches desperately in all directions, and in vain. To the right, low in the black sky, the sun is visible and yet gives no light. It is a sun of faith, a willed sun overpowered by the darkness and still holding its place, waiting, keeping faith in powerlessness. The small flower is not dismayed. In an unmistakably anthropomorphic gesture, it raises its leaf hands in prayer, it raises its flowerhead in trust. The praying hands do not implore, but rather seem to jubilate. Incredibly, the flower almost orchestrates a hymn of jubilation. Like a conductor, the leaves rise to summon invisible players and singers. However black the sky, the flower is totally assured of life's essential joy. Silently, as it lifts up those hopeful leaves, it appears to draw into being a cloud of luminous vapour. Only where the flower is, in the presence of its trustful prayer, is the radiance apparent. Perhaps Kiff suggests that there can be no total darkness for the believing heart? Out of nothingness, light will arise, almost of its own accord. The darker the background, the drearier the prospect, the brighter shines the faith and hope of the believing heart. It calls on a strength not its own – a far stronger creature, the tree, has succumbed. No, it is at peace and in joy because prayer is the certainty of God's love, and with that as our happiness we can live confidently under a darkened sun and in a desolate universe.

Watercolour, 17.7 × 43.8 cm

40

François Boucher

LA TOILETTE, 1742

"What is the meaning of life?
This is the question of all time."

Boucher seeks to please, to charm us with his erotic elegances, to froth the laces of life and twirl its silks. Yet there is more moral bite to him than we suppose. This pretty little creature getting up in the morning does not have by accident a cat stretched out between her outstretched legs, an animal proverbial for its self-centredness, here at play with a ball because there is no mouse to torment and kill. The room's disorder comes from something deep within her psyche, a refusal to conform. There is a candle wastefully burning though the sun shines, there are screens concealing on both sides; we note there are two cups on the tray (hidden lust?), and the half-obscured picture on the wall is a self-portrait (hidden vanity?). The maid is there to serve, and we wonder if the whole world is not seen here as a service world, serving the ego, which sees all things as its possession and for its own gratification. Living for self is animal-like, we can deduce. It is a hidden animality, concealing and screening an egocentricity that leads only to interior disorder. The scene appears somehow theatrical because it is only a pretence life, shallow and ultimately, like the fire, a dying thing. To concentrate upon the self is to opt for triviality. Yet we can evade the knowledge of what we are doing and see only its outer charm. The whole picture is a summons to examination of conscience, to looking beneath our surface patterns, really to waking up and washing – the one item of "la toilette" the little lady seems to overlook.

Oil on canvas, 52.5 × 66.5 cm

Jules Olitski

JUDITH JUICE, 1965

"Real love brings out the 'otherness' of the beloved."

Olitski, born in 1922, is a second-generation American abstractionist, and like Rothko and several others, was born in Russia. Something of that Slavic intensity seems present in his huge colour-field stained work, at once mysterious and seductively beautiful. We could almost say that *Judith Juice* is "about" intensity. We are drawn into that great central oblong of profound, radiant, concentrated blue. Yet it is not a fanatic concentration. The picture breathes, the intense blueness allows for a shimmering white along its central borders, and it lives in contentment with the equally intense orange on three sides. Not only is there coexistence, but there is that silent mutual acceptance that makes the colours each more themselves, more totally focused, because of the complementary hue beside it. The blue is what draws from the orange all its capacity for orangeness, the orange makes the blueness total.

The passion for God that arises from prayer – and can only arise there, where God takes possession and loves within us – is never a narrowing passion. It does not drive out our other desires, but integrates them and makes them absolute in their truth. *Because* God is all that matters, *therefore* everything else at last begins to matter as it should. Love becomes universal, not only allowing others their own truth-to-self but actively helping them to attain it. Freedom, warmth, a security so vast that it can take all risks and not see them as frightening: all this is the result of an absolute directedness to God and God alone. But it is a passion of directedness that exists in *being*, not in feeling. *Judith Juice* is not proclamation, a statement or an appeal: it is an actuality, a painting that one man brought slowly and surely into existence. It is our actions, the life that we lead, that make actual the intensity that God silently draws from us in prayer. Yet not so much "from us": rather it is all from Him, and we are the recipients rather as the canvas is of the artist's paint and energies. Our part is to want: to let God have the time and whatever of our wills we can manage to offer Him. He will do the rest. Prayer is above all a tremendous act of hope, with perhaps no visible sign on which we can depend for comfort. It is God's business: we surrender in trust to Him.

Acrylic on canvas, 244 × 172 cm

Martha Alf

FOUR PEARS NO. 3, 1986

"What beauty we pass by without a thought!"

For years Martha Alf has deliberately chosen the simplest of media – coloured pencil on paper – and the simplest of objects, fruit, especially pears, and rolls of paper, especially toilet rolls. Her aim is to show the transcendent beauty, the nobility, of what we pass by without attention. The toilet roll is a perfect cylinder, a monolithic shape of great dignity seen with the reverence of an artist. The pears too are revered and loved. Alf caresses them into being, letting the clear light of the Pacific coastland play over all their curves and declivities. When she has wholly summoned the pears into fullness of being – a lovely symbol for how prayer summons all our potential into actuality, God's light creating us into beauty – Alf then investigates the relationships between the individual pieces.

Man was not made to live alone. Community is a need, a God-given need that both purifies and completes us. The relationships between Alf's pears are not specifically anthropomorphic. The fruit does not change into men and women, but there *is* a relationship and we are drawn to perceive it. In this study, we see two pears in mutual dependence (one more than the other), with a third involved but separate. The fourth pear leans yearningly towards the group, separated and unable to approach. No moral judgement is made – or seen as possible. But we are called to look at our own community relationships, where we stand and how we view the stance of others. Have we the tenderness and reverence towards them that Alf depicts here?

Coloured pencil on paper, 35.5 × 43 cm

Malcolm Morley

ARIZONAC, 1981

"To be alive is to be at risk."

The great thing in art, as in life, is to maintain the freedom and intensity of passion with the balance of wise order. Malcolm Morley achieves both by first painting in watercolour with a free wild concentration of power. Then he squares off the paper and translates the image to canvas, unifying it into a profound statement while preserving its archaic force.

Arizonac is an unsettling picture. The models for the god figures were Mexican dolls, semiidols with fertility symbols in their hands. The gods, the "unreal" figures, are painted with solidity and dominate the canvas. Far below them, swallowed in the swirls and obscurity of the volcanic desert, a tiny cowboy, the "real" figure, is almost annihilated to our vision.

Perhaps Morley is signifying that what looms largest may not be what is most real. Our fears take on giant status. They terrify us with their detailed intensity. Yet they are constructions of the imagination, and while we are obsessed with their presence, we may overlook the realities – the volcano is erupting, the cowboy, the human, is alone and deserted. Where are our true concerns? Do we see what Jesus sees or what the heart imagines?

Only in prayer can God draw us into a fiery commitment that is never fanatical. Left to ourselves, we overbalance: too simple, too dovelike in our directness and white hot zeal, our passionate flight to Him – or too complex, too serpentine in our prudent weighing of choices and refusal to risk. Our desert, our Arizona of the heart, must have space for both elements: giant determinations and gentler contextualizing of them. We cannot do this on our own. We pray to be consumed with "the zeal of thy house" which "eats up" human pride and vain fear and lets us stride forward in the peace of Jesus.

Oil on canvas, 203 × 267 cm

Georg Baselitz

MMM IN G UND A, 1961/62/66

*"Wholeness comes about by letting Him pull our
wholeness into being during prayer."*

Baselitz, together with Anselm Kiefer, is one of the recognized giants of contemporary art, not only in Germany but worldwide. Like Francis Bacon, a third giant, he supremely marries abstraction and realism in a uniquely personal manner. Baselitz preserves the human figure which he sees as always central, but he paints it abstractly, so that we see, not the familiar lines of the body, but a composition based upon this. He either inverts his painting with an upside-down image, or, as here, cuts his canvas visually in two so that the halves are not aligned.

MMM, as a figure, is as heroic as his magniloquent initials suggest. He looms gigantic in the vague washes of an indeterminate background. Yet his hands dangle helplessly, his feet seem clumsily blocked by what we at first take to be a dark boulder. But on closer examination we understand his agony and inertia. The boulder is a huge decapitated head, a sinister obstacle to any further progress. The man, barely coherent as a human form, upper and lower torso most fragilely united, can only look heavenward for help. Perhaps significantly, he turns his lumbering back from a blurred vignette of death and slaughter where only the impacted sword is clearly visible.

"G" und "A" probably refers to music tonality and there may be a suggestion of tonal incoherence. (English speakers can read it as a reference to Germany and Austria – Baselitz is bilingual.) Baselitz, like Kiefer, has taken on himself the weight of post-war Germany, fragmented and dishonoured. In taking the weight, he sacrifices it, accepting it as God-given purification. *MMM in G und A* speaks to us of our own fragmented and dishonoured selves. Only in Jesus are we whole, free and active. The deadhead of our past will always block us if we progress in the ego. But true prayer is in Jesus. The awareness of what we are or have been is a summons to turn from self to Him. Discouragement is the response of the ego – trust and joy the response of the Jesus self that will eventually heal us and unite us. *MMM* is a symbol of prayer: a waiting upon God, in love.

Oil on canvas, 195 × 145 cm

Allan McCollum

FIVE PERFECT VEHICLES, 1985–86

"Growth in wisdom is seeing what our preconceptions are."

Allan McCollum is a young New Yorker who satirizes with such elegance that irony becomes beautiful. A "vehicle" is a carrier, a container, an instrument for conveyance – and these vehicles are perfect in the Latin sense *perfectus*, filled to the brim, completed. But what they are filled with, what they carry and contain, is themselves, since they are solid plaster. Not only can the "lid" not be removed, but there is no space within to be opened. Potty pantechnicons for self-conveyance, carriers of self-identity yet the vehicles appear in the likeness of a normal jar or container. Their round forms and the delicate presence of their colour all mask a profound deceit because every artistic device has been employed to make them appear to be what they are not.

The idea is essentially terrifying: the dichotomy between our real selfishness and our outward likeness as human, those creatures made to be receptive of God. McCollum makes the profound morality of the parable acceptable by sheer beauty. We delight in his half-humorous jars, with their policeman-like helmets and portly solemnity. Yet at some level we must hear what the Perfect Container is saying. How prepared are we to be emptied, to be perfect in the Jesus sense, a container for God, for prayer, for love? How radically will we allow Him to scoop out our self-stuffed fullness, to drill into our impacted pride, to chisel off our sealed helmet-heads, to let in the light which will fill us with His Spirit?

Enamels and acrylics on solid-cast hydrocal,
50 × 22 cm each. Installation

Karl Korab

PENDEL, 1985

"Silence is completion of sound, not its absence."

Karl Korab's still lifes and landscapes, though not all as dark as *Pendel*, have the same haunting power. They are like a voice speaking with solemnity and power, but in a language we cannot "understand". We cannot but respond, but it is impossible to discern with clarity what we respond to exactly. In *Pendel*, we are gazing at some strange array of objects that have no apparent function. Korab chooses them for their shape and colour, for their mysterious rightness in combination – in a word, for *themselves*. This ability to appreciate without any reference to use, function or self-involvement, is a visual parable: we are loved like this by God, and called to love our neighbour in the same absolute fashion. It is impossible without prolonged prayer. Korab has looked and looked, sought for light and pattern and so can believe in his still life and show it to us with sacramental dignity.

Even more impressive spiritually, is the pendulum, from which it takes its title. Piero della Francesco has a large ostrich egg pendulum in one of his greatest altarpieces, and something of the spiritual weight of that picture is captured here. Korab's pendulum, however seems very small, yet we have nothing against which we can measure it. It simply hangs there, motionless, a still centre giving meaning to all its context. This interior stillness, this hanging silently on the Will of God, this total dependence, isn't this what prayer is about? Jesus calls us to share in His world, to be its focal point in Him (never, of course, in self), and yet to have no share, to hang "above", gleaming with His light, detached and yet concerned. Again, only He can make our wayward noisy heart into His Pendel, and to do so is His greatest joy.

Oil on canvas, 125 × 126 cm

Andrzej Jackowski

THE TOWER OF COPERNICUS, 1980

"The life and death struggle is to become wholly 'there'."

Jackowski's parents were refugees from Poland, and he spent his early life in a refugee camp, living in the kind of wooden hut he often has in his paintings. It is clearly an image of great emotional significance for him, though the wheeled hut actually came from a photograph he saw of a concentration camp. Its smallness, its poverty, its lack of foundation: all express for him his own state of exile and that of all men, all dwelling in this "vale of tears". Everything Jackowski paints affects us with extraordinary significance. The wild-eyed cat in this picture is both animal and symbol: it seems to stand for Copernicus himself, that Polish monk who truly used his eyes to see and, like the cat, climbed high. That Copernicus built a tower from which better to contemplate the skies is historically verified, but Jackowski's tower does not exist in the world of history. We see only the top of the ladder that must be climbed, and equally, we catch only a glimpse of the heavens towards which that climb is made. The picture encloses us with mystery, with sacrifice, with faith.

All prayer is a climbing, a moving resolutely away from distraction, a seeking for the heavens. Prayer demands labour. But once we have laboured, and done our part of preparation, once we have entered into the Tower, there is no "reward" necessarily. No heavens may blaze upon us. We may feel ourselves in mystery, with the beasts and the rough wooden utensils of our humanity. The glory of prayer is not that it shows us the stars and enriches us experientially, but that we surrender all expectation and leave all to God. What will He show us? What will He do to us? We stand bare in our Tower and allow Him to be totally God.

Oil on canvas, 136.3 × 117 cm

56

Edward Hopper

HOTEL ROOM, 1931

"We can only see His Face in others if we have gazed
long at His Face in prayer."

Hopper is the great painter of loneliness. The woman sits alone, anonymous in the anonymity of a hotel room. She has kicked off the constraints of her high-heeled shoes, tossed onto a shelf the bravado of her fashionable hat, which vaguely recalls an officer's cap. Now, defenceless in the brilliant sunlight, she slumps on a bed which seems rock hard beneath the pressure of her unclothed thighs. She looks without interest at what is in her hands while her bags stand still packed and an empty day is still far from sunset. All around is sterile, surgically clean, almost judgmental in its clarity. Hidden from all eyes, friendly or hostile, the tired solitary woman drops all masks and accepts listlessly. This kind of acceptance of loneliness is born of unbelief. Hopper feels only compassion for such waste, but he sees it very clearly as the tragedy it is. To be alone is to be exposed, not to loneliness, but to God. We are profoundly cherished, all our thoughts and movements of immense interest to Him. Nothing in us can be sterile, unwanted, dull. If we imagine a lover in this room, an ardent concern enwrapping the woman, drawing out from her life and eagerness, we can gauge what God is to the celibate or the lonely. Always there, always vitally interested, always seeking only what is good for us, never expecting us to cope alone, caring, caressing, revivifying. All this poor woman lacks is ours – if we pray, if we accept in faith that we are totally loved by a silent unseen God.

Oil on canvas, 152.4 × 165.7 cm

Joan Mitchell

"Art like prayer is always the expression of longing."

Joan Mitchell was one of the so-called second generation abstract expressionists, and the overallness of *Two Sunflowers* might bring Jackson Pollock to mind. But her work has a profound awareness of nature, of earth, leaf and flower and is only abstract in a poetic sense. We cannot here "see" the two sunflowers, yet they are physically very present. That richly glowing gold, that virginal supportive green, those squiggles of black – all sunflower in colour, all somehow directed upwards, as the flower is, a proud tall radiance which is experienced as a giving thing. The flower does not only seek the sun, it acts like it, it rays out its petals from an intense centre and offers its brightness to those who approach. All these delicate qualities Mitchell makes present to us in this painting.

Yet we would not know this is "two sunflowers" had we not been given the title. The actual canvas is an intricate mesh of colour and line: an abstraction. Given the name, we can read it with joy. Isn't this part of the delight of the work? We have to respond to it, be still before it, let it speak to us, before we can "see". Doesn't this parallel what happens in prayer? We have the words of our faith, we know its concepts and teachings, but we may not see the quick-moving blur of our lives, as *actually lived*, as revealing or even containing those spiritual truths. Yet all God has given us in Jesus is present in the actuality of our day. That is how He comes, first and most in the Mass, but then throughout the day. In prayer we are still, we can allow the jumbled pattern – not to unravel into clear shapes – but to reveal in the very jumble that Jesus was present. And He is present above all as Sun, His radiance, His life-giving warmth, His enlightenment, all come to us in the confusion of activity. He shines within all we are and do, not just to be Sun for us ourselves, but to make us His sunflower, His visible sign to others of what love means. But we first have to see how and where this is happening, and prayer both readies us to be alert and generous during the day, and also holds us exposed to His Presence in itself. It is not just or even primarily, perhaps not at all, our minds that will see our Sun, but our longing hearts, not in any emotional felt sense, but in an existential emptiness that chooses to receive all from Another rather than strive to produce it from within. Spiritual poverty, longing for God, surrender to His presence: all prayer attitudes, all proclaiming Jesus as pure Sun to us.

Diptych, oil on canvas, 279 × 361 cm

Mary Newcomb

THE FAST WALKER, 1984

"The depth of prayer depends on the fidelity of longing."

The Fast Walker surges up at us, almost on top of us before we have quite adjusted to his nearness. But he is unaware. His eyes are half-shut with the intensity of his concentration. Not a runner, not a contestant in any athletic games, it suggests: no, this is a walker, one who practises the same form of locomotion that we do ourselves. We do not all feel able to run, but we all walk. Yet this man focuses on his walking. He is dressed for it, stripped down so as to walk fast. Yet he does not choose his path, it would seem, but takes what comes. He is walking through dense meadow land, wild flowers on every side. He bends his mind and all his psychic energies on walking well, walking fast.

Mary Newcomb gives us a lovely parable of prayer. Outside of prayertime the flowers and the sunshine are there to be admired. But when we settle to prayer, to God's time, then all that matters is to be there as wholly as we can. We certainly do not walk – any movement must come from God – nor is speed an issue. But the attitude of the fast walker, prepared beforehand for his walk, intent only on doing it well, looking neither to right nor to left: all this applies. In prayer, we do not know where we are going except in the vaguest sense: we are motionless before His holy Presence and He can take us where He chooses. We know – because of God's goodness – that our poor attempt to pray is never wasted. We shall always come out of prayer different from when we started, but how and in what way we are different only God can tell. But as the walker here seems almost to be drawn through the grass, attracted magnetically to a goal he cannot see, so are we drawn by grace closer and closer to the Father. He does the drawing and He sees what happens. We close our eyes like the walker and entrust ourselves to the deed: the prayer.

Oil on canvas, 91 × 76 cm

62

Mary Newcomb 84

Ken Kiff

MAN GREETING WOMAN, 1965–66

"Peace is the fruit of total trust."

When Kiff left art school, he entered upon what he calls "a nothingness period", an artistic and personal dark night. Kiff came through it with the help of a Jungian psychotherapist, and embarked upon an almost unclassifiable kind of art. It is both alarmingly simple, innocent to the heart, and yet bears a great weight of psychic power. He painted and repainted *Man Greeting Woman*, seeking, as in most of his works, to express opposites, even opposition, and to reconcile them into unity. The centre of the picture is the man, because Kiff himself is male, and the humble, almost infantile forms of both creatures prevent us seeing any macho emphasis in this. The eye of the man (the "little man" who appears so often in Kiff's work, his symbol for himself and all mankind summed up in his weakness) is the centre of an invisible, almost, circle that curves to include the woman's body. They see themselves as separate, as distanced, as needing to make gestures of greeting and response. In reality, says Kiff, they are intimately joined. He paints "love, acceptance [some people would say they are the same thing and perhaps that's true] and . . . simplicity". What the quotation suggests becomes evident in the picture. Love and acceptance demand simplicity, that uncluttered grace would allow man and woman, the two sides of the self, to be naked to each other and to be reconciled into a perfect circle by the Creator. The comic hat, too big for the man, anchors this magic world in quotidian reality. It makes it clear that the acceptance, the love, *can* happen. Whether it will, depends on how resolutely we enter into Jesus, allowing His Prayer to strip us of accretions and reveal us, shrimp-pink and infantile, vulnerable yet defended, not by pride, but by grace. It is a picture of total trust.

Oil, tempera and gesso on board, 122 × 152 cm

Xavier Valls

SMALL TABLE, YELLOW CERAMIC AND STONEWARE
WITH LAUREL LEAVES, 1988

"Silence is passionate."

Xavier Valls has been classed with Vermeer and Chardin as a poet of silence. His art is totally pure, totally still, totally attuned to the music of God that to us is holy silence. It is a gentle celebration of the mystery of ordinary and simple realities, of their secret depths and beauty which only the long slow gaze of the praying heart can see.

Here we have a small table; we do not see the ground on which it stands and all round it are not walls and other furniture but a pale luminosity that bathes it in light. To the artist, the very being of this small kitchen object of utility is mysterious. He has to isolate it, to look at it with reverence and love. On it stand three objects. We are told in the title what two of them are: a yellow bowl and a stoneware jar holding laurel leaves. The bowl is radiant, a pure and heavenly yellow. But what is within it? Are those two spatulas we see, and do they rest on anything? They stay there quietly, conserving their secret. The pale stoneware too holds its secret: is the laurel merely held within, as we would expect – cut leaves therefore – or is a plant growing there? The proud virility of the laurel suggests that it grows and flourishes. But Valls does not feel we need to know. Just in what it is, the combination of smooth stone and free wild leaf is beautiful. And finally, there is the strange third object, a precious seeming box, where the light gleams as if reflected in gold and the lid has a roughness indicating patterning or jewelwork. What is the golden box doing with the ceramic dish and its suggestions of working tools, or the laurel in its jar? We do not know. Can we not delight in what we are shown without a restless striving after explanation? Valls is content to contemplate, to love without reasoning, to accept things on their own terms whether he understands them or not. God accepts us like this, only He, of course, does truly understand. But He allows us to be in all our diversity. We know we are being drawn closer to Him in prayer when we also simply accept, and love, and allow all in our life to unfold its beauty in the light of God's Presence.

Oil on canvas, 116 × 89 cm

Canaletto

WARWICK CASTLE: THE EAST FRONT, 1752

*"Things that just seem to happen are really leadings
of this Spirit."*

All his life Canaletto painted essentially only two things – the mass of great architecture and light shining on it. Since he lived nearly all that life in Venice, he also delighted in light shining on water, but during his stay in England he made do very happily with light and its shadow on the surroundings of great buildings. It is always the exterior that attracts him: those vast strong towers lofting majestically into the blueness of a rather Venetian-looking sky, the solid whiteness of the castle walls, their complexity, their insolence of security almost compared to the bright and miniscule humans who stand without. But those humans, or others like them, built this castle, and the same light bathes all impartially, uniting the long-lasting stone and the short-lived flesh.

As human creatures, we are all builders, building our lives, building our happiness. But perhaps this picture suggests that we "know not what we do". We are somehow "outside": what lies within is not ours to know. We "build", in prayer, for God. It is His castle, He lives inside it and knows its rooms and beauties. All that is solid and true in our lives comes from Him and is far more His than our own. We need only carry on with our duties and pleasures under the shade of the prayer-castle He has made for us. "Unless the Lord builds, in vain do the builders labour", says the Psalm. Let Him build us a prayer-castle, and let us be content to live "without", praying for His sake and not our selfish own. Let us live in the light which is so visibly not our own.

Oil on canvas, 73 × 112 cm

Rainer Fetting

SLEEPING NUDE ON SOFA, 1986

"You can't take life seriously unless you take it with joy."

Rainer Fetting is one of the group of "Wild Artists" that rose to prominence in Berlin some years ago. They are all young men deeply affected by the insecure and divided state of their city, and their art is expressionist in the true German tradition – intense personal emotion intensely expressed. But Fetting has matured into a painter who expresses far more than his own personal fears and griefs. He shows us reality, but only at a distance; it is wholly transformed by the artist's imaginative love. Fetting loves what he paints, sees it as heroic, larger and more exotic than life but thereby more true to what life potentially can be. Here his *Sleeping Nude on a Sofa* is far removed from a domesticated milieu. We can barely make out the sleeping body, only just enough to see it is a body, a large male form whose face the painter veils. The veiling is deliberately revealed as the painter's by a large red mask. Fetting is not concerned with the individual but with man, with Adam, only this Adam still awaits the enlivening Finger of God. The sofa could be read as a flowering meadow were we not told differently, and the far wall of the room looks like a dark and light-filled sky. In other words, literal truth is here but transformed. Its potential beauty is set free, given voice to sing: we are called to praise the nobility of man and his surroundings.

The eye that sees nobility and beauty in what another would regard as ordinary is the eye of prayer. Only in the light of Jesus can we see the fullness of creation. Nothing small, sordid, drab, all glorious and infinite in possibility. Love draws these qualities into being, so that we can never again see merely the littleness of life but only, because of God, its greatness.

Oil on canvas, 130 × 180 cm

Shanti Panchal

WAGH IN PURPLE SHAWL, 1983

*"He is the leader of the dance; the steps in prayer and
life are His."*

Shanti Panchal is a young Indian artist who now lives in Britain but creates from
his memories of his village childhood. He tells us the minimum, just enough for
us to respond to the silent secret people he sets before us. Wagh is a dark enigma.
He is exposed to our view externally full in the front of the painting, darkly
brooding in his purple shawl, seated upon the regal muted crimson of the sofa.
He is hemmed in by the green armchair, imprisoned in the amplitude of his
shawl. Only the black head broods out, and not at us. No one can take his
privacy from him, no swathing can impair the interior freedom that makes him
a man. All that is outer, whatever its significance or strength, Panchal suggests,
leaves the essential self untouched. Panchal shows us something of human dignity, its independence of anything but God. "If God be for us, who is against
us?" To accept the frustrations of human living, its lack of scope, the binding
effect even of its sweeter elements, its purple shawls, its blank background, to
accept all this without self-pity but with hope, looking to God for our salvation
and our freedom, that is what prayer is meant to achieve within us. If we hold
ourselves silent before God, even if the silence is constricted and coloured by
factors we cannot control, then He comes to free and fulfil. We do not need to
see any of this. We may always feel straitjacketed by our personality – Wagh
is clearly a melancholic fellow – hemmed in by our environment or heredity,
imprisoned by our past weaknesses and sins. How we feel is unimportant. God
is a God of soaring freedom but He can only lift into His peace a heart that
allows itself to be still before Him, and trust, to be afraid and helpless and yet
at peace, because what is deepest within us *knows* that His Presence is Salvation.

Watercolour on paper, 96.5 × 76 cm

Eric Fischl

TIME FOR BED, 1981

"We are loved out of sinfulness if we let Him."

At first sight, we may find Eric Fischl unappealing, with his acid colours and disturbing subject matter. Yet the sexuality with which he is so often concerned is essentially a symbol for love, God's love, and though we may never come to like him, he is always worth attention.

Here we see a family, not one of whom looks at another. Their unity is merely spatial: they occupy the same room. The father turns his back on them all, gaunt and ravaged with his private misery. That he stands before a piano and yet has only one arm suggests impotence, sexually and even humanly: he is engulfed in despair. Although his wife clings to him, it is not to him as a person but as a thing, a possession which, vampirelike, she devours. The glass she carelessly holds at his throat suggests a blood-draining: she nibbles his finger, and behind her gross, avid body can be seen the shadows of previous victims. Her sin is greed, selfishly intent only on self. The adolescent son is pathetically clad in a Superman outfit, his narrow wretched form a mute testimony to his inability to fulfil what is expected. His hand cups his genitalia in a spasm of fear. Sexuality, adulthood, successful maturity – the demands of life terrify him and his fear makes even movement impossible. The little sister, on the contrary, is happy to move, acting out her fantasies, dolled up for the night and isolated in unreal dreams of her future. She is not yet old enough to understand the unhappiness for which she is busy preparing herself.

Lest we attribute this solitary grieving to the family's station as wealthy and civilized, Fischl gives them a tribal sculpture in their room. Here is primitive man in his massive nakedness, yet he too is despairing. The African figure clasps its hands fearfully around life's cup, and it too cannot "look" at another.

All these individuals are facets of the self. We also are mutilated, greedy, afraid, unreal. But the love that will heal our mutilations, fulfil our longings, answer all our hopes, lead us radiantly into truth – this love we possess in Jesus. Jesus is the answer, the living love that finds the lonely man and binds him into family. We have only to open the eyes of our prayer and Jesus is there for us.

Oil on canvas, 183 × 244 cm

74

Paul Klee

FULFILMENT ANGEL, 1920

"Actions fuelled by prayer have the radiance of prayer."

Like the pillar of cloud by day and of fire by night, an angel is the symbol that God's people do not journey alone across life's desert: always with them is the tender Presence of the Holy One, made visible in the angel, God is present as all-encompassing Love. Hence Klee shows us a border of tender red, Love's symbolic colour, and the centre of the picture is a heart. A small red sun is seen beneath the angel's wing, to show that love soars high above all earthly lights and splendours. But the angel is also enclosed by the outline of the slab that traditionally represents the Ten Commandments: love is only love in the context of obedience. It is not what we choose to do that matters, it is what God asks us to do. He will always make His loving will known; the angel is clearly intent on service, yet we can scarcely distinguish what precisely that service is. (Does he carry a tray with a watering can? A teapot?) He bears a plaque, though, with Klee's name on it, and perhaps the artist is trying to tell us that love cannot be too exactly determined. It comes from response, and the how and the where and the when will depend on what is being asked. Like the angel's, our eyes must be wide open, wholly intent on seeing what is asked and who asks it. So egoless is *Fulfilment Angel* that we can hardly see him; he flutters in gentlest outline, wings aquiver as he responds to love. At the end of his life, exiled, disgraced, dying, rejected, Klee again and again returned to this symbol. His last angels are wounded and mutilated, suffering angels but always angelic, always symbols of God's holy Presence. Fulfilment angel, fulfilment in God, means this selfless willingness to be used, to serve, to respond without the self-certainties of any outline of duties except that of obedience. Jesus is our angel, our fulfilment, our visible Presence of the Father, and He sends us to be His presence, His fulfilment, to our brothers and sisters.

Lithograph/watercolour, 19.8 × 14 cm

1920 91   Klee

Agnes Martin

ANNOUNCEMENT FOR RECENT PAINTINGS EXHIBITION, 1985

"The asceticism of love is infinite watchfulness."

One cannot deny that this looks like merely a gallery announcement, and so, of course, it is. But the announcement is made on an Agnes Martin painting and virtually leaves its essence untouched. Agnes Martin is the most pure and delicate of any contemporary artist. She has something of that angelic sensibility that gave Fra Angelino his name, and is well called "Agnes": Lamb. Her paintings are minimal art, art at its most exquisite. Here she has merely taken a pure white canvas and on it drawn, at minutely irregular intervals, lines of varying thicknesses and strengths. No colour, no image, nothing *happening* in the whole artwork: just those tender lines dividing its expanse. In such an emptiness of action, the smallest difference becomes of interest.

Isn't this gentle painting an image of prayer? We are simply there for God to possess us. Motionless before Him, the least stirring of the heart becomes clear, the least insight or impulse to generosity is seen and noted. Our lives, all too easily a mishmash of half-recognized motives, straighten out into simplicity. "Speak, Lord, your servant is listening." We hear nothing, but the silent word will leave its impress. All our activity is to be present, not to distract ourselves with deliberations, to let God possess all we are in whatever way He pleases. The steady faith that keeps us surrendered is the equivalent of Martin's faith in the visual power of a simple straight line, seen in truth.

Her work grows on us slowly, perhaps, but no artist is more truly contemplative.

White vellum, 15 × 12.5 cm

AGNES MARTIN

RECENT PAINTINGS

18 October - 16 November 1985

PREVIEW OF THE EXHIBITION
THURSDAY 17 OCTOBER 6-8 PM

MARGO LEAVIN GALLERY

812 NORTH ROBERTSON LOS ANGELES 90069 213 273-0603

Gordon Matta-Clark

"The dance of Joy takes place over the tomb."

Matta-Clark was not exactly an Earth artist nor yet an Installation artist, yet his works partook of the nature of both. What he did was to take over a building that was to be demolished, and while it still stood, slice it, rearrange it, use it to express a truth and a vision. The "work" could be entered and "experienced", and before it was destroyed, he recorded it in photographs. One can only imagine what the actual experience was like but the photographs are strangely impressive.

His usual choice was of buildings that he felt had restricted their occupants, depriving them of light and freedom. To slice and open out these seemingly impermeable structures was an act of great daring, an inconceivable rearrangement of what stood as solid immutability. He was trying to tell us that our lives are as free, as light-filled, (as Jesus-filled), as we *choose them to be*. No structure can possibly wall in the desiring heart. "The prayer of the just man shall pierce the cloud," says Scripture. Matta-Clark shows it piercing the roof and walls, opening what seemed for ever shut, unlimited in its potential because not reliant on its own strength: In God, all things are possible.

Here he has photographed some kind of shed, some factory dimly lit. He has carved a half-circle in the wall, and the photograph enshrines the moment when the setting sun blazes in its fullness through the opening. Only for one short period of the day will the sun be so captured, but the strange heavenly segment will remain even in its absence, reminding us of what is possible.

Into the constriction of our lives, prayer must carve an aperture for God. We may wait in patience, never "seeing" the glory invading the space we prepare for Him, but He always comes, seen or unseen. Our task is to open out the space, to keep it open, to keep watch before it, never to forget that His sunlight wants only to irradiate us and cannot be restrained, except by deliberate choice.

The picture is of pure hope, that essential virtue which we don't sufficiently value. Hard work, to be hopeful, but what a recompense!

Installation

Mali Morris

"Only eyes that have sought Him in prayer see
His presence in the day."

Mali Morris (born 1945) has said that for her, growth as a painter has meant growth into freedom. She no longer restricts or constricts herself, but approaches each new canvas as open to inspiration as she can be. She tries to cling only to her own inner truth, to a sensibility sharpened by years of effort to be receptive. Nor does she restrict this receptivity to the time actually spent before the canvas. Her day is open to receive whatever insight comes to her.

Perhaps this attitude, so profoundly akin to that of one who prays, is made visible in *A Vision of the Mermaids*. Not *her* vision, implies Morris: in fact, we get the impression that the painter does not "understand" the picture any more than we do. Mermaids are another species, creatures of the imagination, born to an atmosphere different to our smoke-polluted air. We could almost equate mermaids with angels in their essential unlikeness to fallen man. What, then, do the Mermaids see in vision? Horizons and verticals of colour, strange seaweed-like whirls and squiggles, all afloat in an almost transparent matrix. All we can or are asked to do is to *receive* this vision, let its beauty move us, be stilled by its motionless peace. We can take from it no concrete word or message.

When prayer is as imageless as this, we can feel it is "wrong". Yet the vision Jesus shows us when we receive Him is as untranslatable into human terms as this vision is. Nothing seems to happen. But it is not *we* who determine the meaning. It is Jesus who prays and Jesus who understands. C. S. Lewis says of the Eucharist that Jesus told us to take and eat, not take and understand. The abstract beauty of a painter like Mali Morris is symbolic of these deep mysteries.

Acrylic on canvas, 62 × 152 cm

Anish Kapoor

UNTITLED, 1990

"He is the eternity that makes our time beautiful."

Anish Kapoor is a sculptor, and he has the rare privilege of having in his background Hindu, Jewish and Christian strains. He draws on all three, seeking that central mystery that gives any religion its power. In his work at the last Venice Biennale, for which he won a prize, he presented great rectangles of stone in which was some central piercing. The viewers looked deep within and saw a secret blueness. This combination of the radiance and the inwardness has fascinated him always. He has created works covered with an intense brightness of coloured powder, both alluring and repelling. The brightness cannot be "touched", it is not for our possessing, yet it persists in presenting itself before us. In his drawings he has explored this concept of the intangible secret at the heart of all reality, and our helplessness to make it our possession and as it were open it up. "Untitled", 1990, shows us a cloudy mass of gold, brown and ochre. The clouds drift and part, thickening as they near the centre. The centre itself is fissured, slit to its depths, by a strange streak of the most vivid blue. Do the darkly golden clouds conceal an expanse of blueness? Or are we seeing the very heart of the vapours themselves, their secret hue? We can never know, we can never be certain whether we are seeing through or seeing into. That is Kapoor's central theme.

All life is potentially prayer. Nothing is meant to be alien to our union with the Spirit of Jesus. We take special time for prayer so as to deepen and make ardent the time outside this, the "ordinary" time when He is equally present to us but we may not be present to Him. Yet this being present of ours cannot be an intellectual awareness, since duty and common sense make demands to which all our concentration must attend. It is the heart that can learn how to be present always, never to leave the holiness of His nearness. "I sleep, but my heart watches", says the Canticle. If we can be in His presence when we sleep, how much more when we wake, and seriously tackle the work or the play that He makes part of our actual living? It is the "how" that concerns us, and that is what Kapoor shows, that mysterious inwardness that is totally real and totally central.

Gouache and ink on paper, 76.5 × 56.5 cm

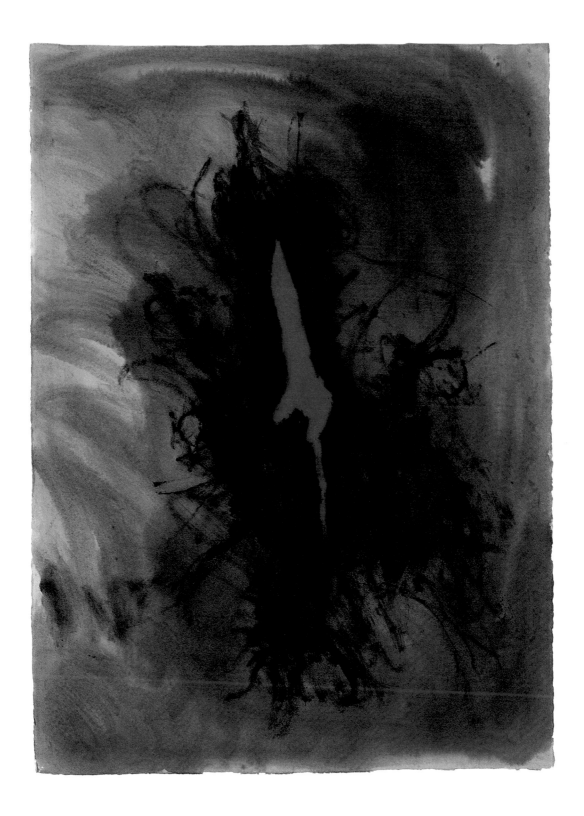

Edward Allington

SNAIL FROM THE NECROPOLIS OF HOPE, 1983

*"We must press close to the Cross to be taken into
the Resurrection."*

Edward Allington's work is always mysterious, and perhaps we can only contemplate it in silence. His deepest urge is to seek for truth, to winnow appearance from reality, to confront dream and illusion and yet salvage the secret longing that has brought them into power and being. A favourite image is the gilded shell, the cornucopia, the spiral of cyclical time, the breast shape, all promising heart's desire yet in our daily practice all pouring forth either false or tainted richness. In this work, the shell is specified as snail shell, the one image we do *not* associate with cornucopic fullness. Even this lowly image, Allington suggests, becomes beautiful when gilded. But this snail has crept forth from the Necropolis of Hope, and so its body is a tremulously united concoction in which are half-dozing winged insects and concealed berries. Hope on earth may dwell in a Necropolis, a city of the dead, because earthly hopes are essentially perishable and deceptive. But from the tombs comes a lowly life form, the slow-moving snail. It has been made from hope's earthly promises – unripe fruit and shortlived insects – but it transforms them into a living creature.

The sculpture could be seen as Patience made spiritual. Like virtue that fully trusts God, ("I know in whom I have believed," says St Paul), it can afford to wait, to be small, to compose its body from all the hopes that come to nothing in this life. True Hope, true Patience, uses the disappointments and disillusionment of living and makes them a means of fulfilment. It ignores appearances, it lives on another plane, that true plane where God "does not delay".

Wood, polystyrene, plaster and plastic insects, 32 × 32 × 68 cm

David Inshaw

"The ordinary is translucent with Jesus."

Inshaw and his friends started the Ruralist Movement some years ago, and all the examples of his work that I've seen are exactly that – rural. But their fascination is in the strange brooding light with which his countryside is filled. The sense of nostalgia for a vanished and pastoral England is piercingly clear, yet with it goes an eerie awareness of Presence. Obviously the Wiltshire landscape has known the presence of man for millennia. Absolutely without drama, independent of the spectator (unless we count the rainbow as such) these simple fields and hedges somehow proclaim that mysterious Power which overwhelmed a poet like Wordsworth. To call this a mystical landscape seems exaggeration. Yet can one not feel that it is more than it appears? The fields *wait*. The furrows *know*. The gentle hill rises to a clump of immemorial trees, and they recognize the Lord. But it lessens the awareness to verbalize it. Perhaps the nearest we can come to it is to say, "Be still and know . . ." This is the landscape of adoration.

Oil on canvas, 48.2 × 64.3 cm

Fred Pollock

ORANGE PATCH, 1989

"Behind every fear is an unused capacity."

Fred Pollock's *Orange Patch* is two feet wide but nearly seven feet long. We have to move along it before we can take it in fully. But it seems to demand movement by its very structure. The great colour forms surge from left to right, blowing along like so many autumn leaves, flowing with unhurried energy until they reach haven at the canvas end, where a great curve of deep brown brackets them into stillness. And even then, errant clouds of crimson and white seem to float up, over the bracket, out into infinity. The "orange patch" of the title is only one among other lovely forms and shades, a way of identifying the work but not in any sense defining it. What is so lovely about this Pollock is the acceptance of each colour and shape by the colour and shape of its neighbours.

"Harmony" suggests a toning down, a subordination for the sake of unity, but that is precisely what Pollock does not show us. Each element is wholly and deeply itself, rich raw colour, unmodulated by any desire or – better - any need to fit in with another. Each is confident that its own truth, of whatever kind, is fully adequate to the demands of love. Shapes are ragged, streaked, undercut, overlain: they accept all the conditions of their being, and simply present themselves in truthfulness. It sounds simple. Like most beautiful achievements it requires the most searching interior honesty. There can be no cheating, no allowing a false pride to "improve" the actuality. But to be what one truly is is possible only for those close to the Holy One. The one quality Jesus claimed as His own, as His identity even, was Truth. "I am the Truth," He said. Truth makes rigorous demands, not only on our love of ease, our sloth, but on our pathetic need to be well thought of by others. And it makes equal demands upon our sensitivity to those others. It is not an inward-turning virtue but one that looks out to see what others need and are expressing in their shapes and colours. The fullness of our own being depends upon realizing that we are made to live in relationships. "It is not good for the human to be alone." Alone we wither, we have no movement. We are part of a certain pattern. It is as though Pollock's areas of colour are actively moving one another along: their very presence serves to energize the canvas, and without each individual, *Orange Patch* would falter to a conclusion. But as it is, because of the artist's inspired handling, the work has no conclusion. It moves forward perpetually.

Acrylic on canvas, 59 × 206 cm

90

Ian McKeever

UNTITLED, 1984

"To be human is to pray."

Ian McKeever is a young Scot, one of the new breed of highly intellectual and philosophical artists whose art – like Pollock's, Newman's, Rothko's, Souis' – is his religious faith, as it were. McKeever paints only landscapes, but with a sophistication that sees them as far more subjective and expressionist than objectively factual. They are his focus, setting him free to be true to his vision. Further, he does not paint on canvas but on the actual material of photographs he has taken tramping through the Highlands. The geographical actuality of these photographs is blurred, and using their patterns as ground, he overpaints with fragmented lines and colour, creating an "inscape", a new reality.

Perhaps this approach is even more clearly seen in this drawing. He says of drawing that it is "rooted, not in what is perceived, but in the act of mark-making, which patterns, arrests and fixes. What is represented is primarily activity. The marks and traces that constitute it are a process of stops and starts, of interacting gestures, punctuated by gaps . . . an activity . . . exposed, through doing . . ." In other words, though landscape may be his starting point, his drawing has not the least intention to represent it, nor to abstract from it. This is Abstract Expressionism at its most stark. He draws "his activity", the secret movement of his being which he cannot explain and, in this one activity, is not asked to control. We are faced with a seismograph of the human mind, exposed, vulnerable, lovely in its unloveliness.

So we at prayer. We have only to be, to let what we most truly are be exposed to the eyes of one who loves us. McKeever courageously exposes himself to the passer-by, hiding only under an expectation of non-understanding. We freely and trustfully "act", without conscious ego when we pray, hiding under nothing because to Him all hearts are exposed. But this exposure can only be made creatively – when we love him. Our first prayer must always be: Lord, *teach* us to pray . . .

Pastel on paper, 41.5 × 30 cm

Anish Kapoor

MOTHER AS A MOUNTAIN, 1985

*"What in practice is being a woman? It is to be
true to one's heart."*

Anish Kapoor is half-Hindu, half-Jewish, both traditions which have a great reverence for the mother figure. His sculptures are essentially sacred objects, to be contemplated less for what they are than for the idea behind them. Yet the numinous can only work on us through the visible, and what is primarily visible, and almost tangible here, are the materials of his work. He has used wood, gesso and pigment, a silent invocation of the powdery pigments used in Hindu festivals. *Mother as a Mountain* is densely coated with red powder, and it spills out in a tide around the base, keeping the viewer at a distance and marking the place out as holy ground. The graffiti on the surrounding walls express the dim strivings and approximations through which he arrived at the awesome stillness of the final figure.

Julian of Norwich tells us that God is our mother and surely He is the primal mother-as-a-mountain. That gracious and regal solemnity that is infinitely protective and infinitely tender, whose beauty is wholly for us, the children. We can never comprehend the holy mountain, but we know that access is not conditional on completeness or indeed on anything but need and desire. The mountain is "open", we came from it and will return to it. Your holy mountain rises in beauty, the joy of all the earth, sings the psalmist. We are too often daunted by the height, the unscalable degree of the folds. We forget that the Mountain is Mother, more desirous to receive and protect us than can be imagined. If the sacredness of its being keeps us at a distance, it does not so keep the Holy Son, Jesus. In Him is our access, our safety. Jesus who called Yahweh "Abba" is He who leads us into the heart of the Mother-Mountain.

Wood, gesso and powder pigment, 145 × 200 × 145 cm

94

Ralph Steadman

BALCONY SCENE, S.E. DALLAS, 1973

"Pain is the fruit of the Tree of Joy."

This is the only picture I've chosen that isn't beautiful, and yet there is a beauty in the controlled ferocity with which Steadman flails at what man has done to his Negro brother. The contempt is only bearable because he directs it, not at us, but at himself, too. We have all collectively caged the Black, like an animal, deformed him, brutalized him by ignorance and poverty. The misshapen apathy with which these three sit solidly behind their wire is a sin of our committing. Yet, degraded and outcast, the Negro looks out with a sorrowful dignity. Who really is degraded, them or us?

And some indescribable depth to the picture makes it seem reversible, too. We treat the Negro like this – and equally, anyone we treat like this is Negro to us. There are those we cast away, deprive of our esteem, our love, whom we don't regard as fully alive and as wonderful in themselves as we ourselves are.

Balcony Scene has a terrible irony. Juliet and her Romeo in the darkness: all men should converse as they do, not seeing clearly, perhaps, but determined on love.

Indian ink and sepia on cartridge paper, 59.6 × 85 cm

96

Orazio Gentileschi

THE REST ON THE FLIGHT INTO EGYPT, c.1620

"We can distance Truths to a fairy-tale romanticism."

What is so astounding about Orazio Gentileschi's picture is its unflinching realism. Many artists have depicted the same scene. They show the Holy Family embowered in welcoming trees, serenaded by circling flocks of angels, bathed in the tender light of imaginative religious fantasy. For them, for this special Family, the art suggests, everything in life must be different from the sad and sordid conditions known to us sinners. But Gentileschi shows a family about which two things are brutally clear: they are very poor, and they are bone weary. One feels that Joseph is too tired even to try to seek shelter for the night; he has unsaddled the ass and fallen exhausted on the baggage. He has not even had the energy left to cover his body against the night chill. Mary has forced herself upright until she has fed her child. Her naked feet stick out ungracefully as he sucks hungrily and almost apprehensively – a big clumsy child, far from the tiny beshawled infant of poetic idealism. The ass hangs heavily over the whole scene, its brooding animal head both repeating the animal reality of the weary human bodies and seeming to make an ironic comment on their frailty. We see three peasants, three refugees, three poor tired creatures who face the hardness of life bravely but without divine protection.

Yet we know they *are* protected, but not against the common lot of humanity. They are protected by their absolute faith in God. They do not have faith that He will make things easy or even possible. We feel that should the energies of the adults fail, and the enemy catch up with them: should Jesus be put to death now, in His babyhood, then still all three would "believe". Jesus would still be our Redeemer. What the Holy Family spell out for us is that all is in the hands of our loving Father. "Though he slay me, yet would I trust in Him," says the Scripture. God brings us to his haven of rest and renewal, but in His way, at His time. We may only feel our fatigue and failure: all the more occasion to trust and lie down, like Joseph, at peace in the divine care, like Mary, intent only on Jesus.

Oil on canvas, 175.3 × 218.4 cm

Robin Philipson

COCKS FIGHTING, 1988

*"The fight between the ego and the Jesus Spirit is
at its sharpest in prayer."*

Sir Robin Philipson was one of the great Scottish colourists, and it is the very
brilliance of the colour here that alerts us to the non-realistic nature of this picture.
This is not two cocks fighting in any literal sense. Philipson has set above the
scene a frieze of ornamental forms to make quite clear the symbolic nature of
what he depicts. The cocks are creatures of the Spirit, duelling to the death, and
to eternal life. It is a fight of intensest passion, each creature needing passionate
concentration and lightning quickness, razor-sharp weapons and unrelenting
determination to kill or be killed. What can these winged creatures be? Many
interpretations are possible – we are left free. But the one I find most congenial
is that we are shown the desperate fight within us of our two deepest desires,
our fundamental attitudes, those which make us human. One is our passion to
be our own god; to subdue everything to the ego, to rely on self and control
our environment. The other – just as fundamental – is our desire to be made
whole in God, to be possessed by Him and set free from the ego – a desire most
people do not see with clarity. The two must fight it out, and *Cocks Fighting*
shows us that the fight is *beautiful*. It has to be: nobody ever reached God without
this combat. It cannot be sidestepped, it cannot be downplayed. Cocks fight
with terrible bloody violence. "The Kingdom of Heaven suffers violence and
the violent carry it away." No need, then, to feel shame at our struggles with
self, only gratitude that we are indeed struggling, and prayer to struggle with
cocklike firmness and intensity. If we weaken, the ego-spirit may stab to the
heart. Prayer is our razor-blade weapon: we do not fight unarmed, though of
ourselves we can never overcome. "Have courage, I have overcome the world."
In prayer, we are made ready for the fight, during prayer the fight is at its
sharpest. To God will belong the holy victory, and, as in this picture, we may
not see it: but we believe.

Oil on canvas, 76 × 91 cm

Larry Cohen

OPEN DOOR-VIEW FROM MALIBU CANYON ROAD, 1987

"Holiness means seeing the world through His eyes."

This is a vertiginous picture, alluring and deceptive. We begin in certainty, at the table with its austere furnishing. The doors are readable, too, one open one shut, beckoning us out. But onto what? The streaked area outside is strangely shadowy; in fact, it seems *only* shadow towards the centre where we can dimly descry the city through the blueness. And beyond: what exactly are we looking at? Do we see roads or rivers, fields or lakes? We can recognize houses and trees, but there are baffling shapes as well, architecturally and naturally, and the long thin shadows have no observable origin. Far in the distance glimmers the sea, validating the claim Cohen makes: this is a view high up on a canyon in California. We accept this essential truth of it while still puzzled, still searching with some anxiety for the legibility of the apparently unproblematic. In the end, we remain unsure.

To see from a height a vast stretch of land is deeply flattering to us: we are contingent creatures that long to be in control, to know what is coming, to possess somehow our present and our future. No wonder the Scripture has the Prince of this world take Jesus up a high mountain to tempt Him. Even if only with our eyes, we want to "possess". And equally no wonder that Jesus stressed to His disciples the need for "littleness". What He meant by "like a little child" is infinitely profound, but one meaning surely is that the little ones cannot see over a distance. They see only what is near, their immediate context, the present minute, as it were. To give up to God our desire to control goes very deep in us. We justify it in so many seemingly spiritual ways. But in giving our present and our future to Him, we really give Him only our desire to control, not any reality. We cannot see ahead, cannot possess or even read the future. As in Cohen's painting, shadows and shapes essentially defy our certitudes. We cannot truly see: God sees – we surrender that right – His already, and commit ourselves in trust. Not only does He see, but He sees in love and wisdom; He can make sense of pure mystery, unite the scattered images of our lives into a pattern that will display to us His beauty. To open the door of our canyon to God is the essence of prayer.

Oil on canvas, 168 × 112 cm

Diego Rivera

THE FLOWER CARRIER, 1935

"Nothing in us is meant to lie infertile."

Mexico has a rich heritage of folk art, and it had an unexpected flowering in the thirties in the Mexican muralists of which Diego Rivera is the best known. Fundamentally a peasant art, it hymned both the nobility and the oppression of the poor in massive and simple forms whose message is unmistakable. A more sophisticated age may decry their oversimplification, but the deepest things are, in fact, simple, and "the mere babes" can see what is hidden from the "wise and learned".

The picture is all strong diagonals and swelling rotundities. Even the flowers are only seen as round flowerheads. The man has become a beast of burden, carrying his load like the ass, while the woman solicitously supports him. There is a clear visual reference to the position of Jesus fallen beneath the Cross as he struggles on to Calvary. Yet the pose of the burdened peasant is tense and active. Any minute now, we know he will spring to his feet and bear off his flowers to the market. If he is clad in humdrum white and yellow (shade and sun), his woman is ripe with full-glowing shades of fertility. She is like a flowering plant herself.

Perhaps the picture speaks to us of love and its responsibility. We must bow down, bend down, submit and let the weight bear down upon us. The humble and obedient heart is not concerned for itself. The burden is for others – for them the flowers and the joy they bring. We are content, if we love Jesus, to take up the yoke and live simply and humbly in its shade. Others will see, as in this picture, a gleaming richness of opulent colour, a rounded beauty, a perfectly balanced pattern. If our part is to help Jesus achieve this and never to experience it ourselves, then blessed the part that He has given us. In heaven, which this overflowing basket symbolizes, the flower carrier will become flower, flower of the field, as Jesus is called in the Canticles. He is flower to us and He will make us flower for Him.

Oil and tempera on masonite, 121.9 × 121.3 cm

Albert Herbert

JONAH AND THE WHALE, c.1988

"Pain has an end: the deepest thing is joy – it is everlasting."

Albert Herbert carries out visually what the Bible does verbally; he tells a story and at the same time shows it has a universal significance, a deep meaning for the spirit searching for God. Here we see Jonah, that archetypal figure of the man or woman who says no to God. God in His desperate love makes him taste the meaning of his no, and he is swallowed by the whale. But the whale – that seems only disaster – carries him safe to dry land. Herbert has a special fondness for the moment when Jonah once again is faced with his vocation, to the full human use of his gifts. Will he accept and step out of the safety of his cetacean haven? The whale snakes across the picture, great mouth agape, to let Jonah make his choice. The comforting belly where he travelled free and protected is not on view. What is on view, painfully so, is poor, naked, frightened Jonah, and the world of responsibility and maturity that awaits him. It is a free world where the animal in us is under control: the goose girl guards the wandering of her goose. There are other people too in this real world, and Jonah will have to cope with the human need to love and be loved. As he is, poised to choose, he is surrounded by the hazy wanderings of the blue-green sea, uncontrollable and resistant to our labour, in all the ways that the stony earth is not. Ease and safety and self-love as opposed to work and risk and self-giving. Like all of us, he finds the cost of being a free full person a heavy one.

But the colours of the picture, gleaming, thick, radiant, tell us something more. Jonah's dilemma is in his own mind. God's love awaits him on every side. If he lifts his eyes in prayer, he will see the sheer beauty of the Love that encompasses him. We are not asked to bear the burden of humanity alone. We are only asked to realize that alone we cannot bear it. God bears it – Jesus draws us into the Spirit of Holiness. Our only task is to ask for His help. How it will come is not our affair. Love may carry us inside a whale or along a stony shore: it may seem anything but what we want. But if we trust our God, if we accept that Jesus knew His Mystery and taught us to call Him Father, then the gleaming beauty that Herbert shows us becomes our vision of life, and there is no more fear.

Oil on canvas, 28 × 35.5 cm

List of Illustrations and Acknowledgements

ALBERT HERBERT *Moses on the Mountain of God*, 1991. Private collection, courtesy of England & Co Gallery.

RAPHAEL (1483–1520) *Altarpiece: The Madonna and Child with Saint John the Baptist and Saint Nicholas of Bari (The Ansidei Madonna)*. Courtesy of the Trustees, The National Gallery, London.

GUERCINO (1591–1666) *The Woman taken in Adultery*. By permission of the Governors of Dulwich Picture Gallery.

REMBRANDT *The Woman taken in Adultery*, 1644. Courtesy of the Trustees, The National Gallery, London.

MICHAEL FINN *Crucifix*, 1985/6. Photograph by Bob Berry.

ANNE GREBBY *Ashes*, 1992. Courtesy of the artist.

LINO MANNOCCI *Isle of the Annunciation*, 1991. Courtesy of the artist.

PETER PRENDERGAST *Dinefwr: Spring*, 1991. Courtesy of Agnews, Bond St., London. Photograph by Jonathan Marsden, courtesy of The National Trust's Foundation for Art and Oriel 31 Gallery.

ODILON REDON *The Mystical Boat (La Barque Mystique)*. Woodner Family Collection, New York. Photograph by Jim Strong.

MARGARET NEVE *Angel in the Sky*, 1987. Courtesy of Montpelier Studio, London.

MARIA CHEVSKA *Living Memory*, 1988. Courtesy of the artist.

MAXWELL DOIG *Welding Mask Behind Metal Plate I and II*, 1991. Courtesy of The Hart Gallery, Nottingham.

ALBERT MARQUET *Sailing Boats at La Rochelle*, 1920. Musée des Beaux-Arts de Lyon. © ADAGP, Paris and DACS, London 1993.

ROBERT NATKIN *Hitchcock Series – Egypt*, 1988. Collection of the artist, courtesy of Gimpel Fils.

KEN KIFF *Flower and Black Sky*, 1987–88. Courtesy of the artist and Marlborough Fine Art (London) Ltd.

FRANÇOIS BOUCHER *La Toilette*, 1742.
Thyssen-Bornemisza Collection,
Lugano. Photograph courtesy of
Artothek.

JULES OLITSKI *Judith Juice*, 1965.
© Jules Olitski/DACS, London/
VAGA, New York 1993. Courtesy of
Salander-O'Reilly Galleries, Inc. NY.

MARTHA ALF *Four Pears no. 3* (for
Frederick Wight 1902–87), 1986.
Courtesy of the artist. Photograph by
Pam Perugi Marraccini.

MALCOLM MORLEY *Arizonac*, 1981.
Courtesy of Mary Boone Gallery, New
York.

GEORG BASELITZ *MMM in G und A*,
1961/62/66. Private collection. Courtesy
of Schloß Derneburg.

ALLAN MCCOLLUM *Five Perfect Vehicles*,
1985/86. Installation: Rhona Hoffman
Gallery, Chicago, 1986. Courtesy of the
artist.

KARL KORAB *Pendel* (Pendulum), 1985.
Courtesy of Galerie Hilger, Vienna.
Photograph by Miki Slingsby, courtesy
of Leinster Contemporary Art.

ANDRZEJ JACKOWSKI *The Tower of
Copernicus*, 1980. Arts Council

Collection, The South Bank Centre,
London. Photograph courtesy of Purdy
Hicks Gallery.

EDWARD HOPPER *Hotel Room*, 1931.
Thyssen-Bornemisza Collection,
Lugano.

JOAN MITCHELL *Two Sunflowers*, 1980.
Private collection. © The Estate of Joan
Mitchell. All rights reserved.
Photograph courtesy of Lennon,
Weinberg Inc, New York.

MARY NEWCOMB *The Fast Walker*,
1984. Private Collection, London.
Photograph courtesy of The Crane
Kalman Gallery.

KEN KIFF *Man Greeting Woman*, 1965–
66. Arts Council Collection, The South
Bank Centre, London. Courtesy of the
artist.

XAVIER VALLS *Small Table, Yellow
Ceramic and Stoneware with Laurel Leaves*,
1988. © ADAGP, Paris and DACS,
London 1993. Photograph by Claude
François, Vevey, Switzerland.

GIOVANNI ANTONIO CANAL, called
CANALETTO *Warwick Castle: The East
Front*, 1752. By permission of the
Birmingham Museum and Art Gallery.

RAINER FETTING *Sleeping Nude on Sofa*, 1986. Courtesy of Raab Boukamel Galleries Limited.

SHANTI PANCHAL *Wagh in Purple Shawl*, 1983. Courtesy of the artist.

ERIC FISCHL *Time for Bed*, 1980. Courtesy of Mary Boone Gallery, New York.

PAUL KLEE *Fulfilment Angel*, 1920/21. Felix Klee Collection. Photograph by Peter Lauri, Bern.

AGNES MARTIN *Announcement for Recent Paintings Exhibition*, 1985. Courtesy of Margo Leavin Gallery, Los Angeles.

GORDON MATTA-CLARK *Day's End*, Pier 52, New York City, 1975. Courtesy of Holly Solomon Gallery, New York.

MALI MORRIS *A Vision of the Mermaids*, 1983. Arts Council Collection, The South Bank Centre, London. Courtesy of Francis Graham-Dixon Gallery.

ANISH KAPOOR *Untitled*, 1990. Private collection, London. Courtesy of the artist. Photograph by Gareth Winters, courtesy of Lisson Gallery, London.

EDWARD ALLINGTON *Snail from the Necropolis of Hope*, 1983. Collection of the artist, courtesy of Lisson Gallery, London. Photograph by Edward Woodman.

DAVID INSHAW study for *She Did Not Turn*, 1974. Private collection. Courtesy of the artist.

FRED POLLOCK *Orange Patch*, 1989. Private Collection. Courtesy of Vanessa Devereux Gallery.

IAN MCKEEVER *Untitled*, 1984. Private collection. Courtesy of Galerie Janine Mautsch, Cologne.

ANISH KAPOOR *Mother as a Mountain*, 1985. Collection Walker Art Center, Minneapolis. T. B. Walker Acquisition Fund, 1987. Courtesy of the artist. Photograph courtesy of Lisson Gallery, London.

RALPH STEADMAN *Balcony Scene, S.E. Dallas*, 1973. Courtesy of the artist.

ORAZIO GENTILESCHI *The Rest on the Flight into Egypt*, c.1620. By permission of the Birmingham Museum and Art Gallery.

ROBIN PHILIPSON PPRSA, RA *Cocks Fighting*, 1988. Photograph courtesy of Michael Le Marchant, Bruton Gallery, Bruton, Somerset.

LARRY COHEN *Open Door-View from Malibu Canyon Road*, 1987. Courtesy of Jan Turner Gallery, Los Angeles.

DIEGO RIVERA *The Flower Carrier*, 1935. San Francisco Museum of Modern Art, Albert M. Bender Collection. Gift of Albert M. Bender in memory of Caroline Walter. Photograph by Ben Blackwell.

ALBERT HERBERT *Jonah and the Whale*, *c.*1988. Private collection, courtesy England & Co Gallery.

The publishers wish to record their gratitude to the artists, galleries, museums and private individuals who have so willingly helped in the preparation of this book by providing transparencies for reproduction or the permission for their use.

Every possible effort has been made to trace copyright or ownership and the publisher regrets any details which are inadvertently omitted or misrecorded.